Also by David Spittle

POETRY:

B O X, (HVTN, 2018)

All Particles and Waves, (Black Herald Press, 2020)

INTERVIEWS:

Light Glyphs (Broken Sleep Books, 2021)

RUBBLES

Spittle

ISBN:

Cover design by Aaron Kent

Edited & Typeset by Aaron Kent

Broken Sleep Books (2022)

Broken Sleep Books Ltd
Rhydwen,
Talgarreg,
SA44 4HB
Wales

Contents

In wizened old terminal birth
I hold up a spalding lemon
is a pearl, is a whizzing point of land's end
laughing at me, and whirling me up
a lap of the goodness

— **Clark Coolidge**

Rubbles

David Spittle

glitter gravel grave

and what you find in place of knowing only *is* if from or for someone else's
story – to welcome the imposter home.
                                                            in the beginning, there were emeralds
that became chipped windscreens that became the glass eyes of long-dead relatives
and there was very little to do about it except notice, on looking back,
that maybe this was the case

and that for some of us – cretaceous radio will catch the waves and

we glitter. gravel. grave.   as brains. abrade. unmade.
honestly. and. and. and. debris takes stock. slugs inhabit the asthmatic easel.

vistas. inner dwindle. whole climates twang.

if. if. is.

then. commotion. as.

interrupting the pleated milk of no lips, flick a brain to revolt – fuck your emailed crumbs, whose baron of your oasis sits its sand upon the tongue? and little me, shucked from neat cup of skull, a plucky nude remonstrating from the bottom of a well as hell hath no fury like thought's seat standing until, like bivalve tenants, bipedal organs trust shivering above the shell [so swears the snow where snow-ware wears the snow] there is nothing here that will save you: no balm, no truth, no reason, no calm before no storm and no forecast from which to drag no bodies from no lake but like crate singing digs the shampoo totally [the sparkle of the possible and the shame of the actual followed by the stink of its burial] a cute-looking squirrel momentarily helps.

oh.   let me light

as past then a song furious and outdoors to slam madrigal like putting your head between a sanding belt and a circular saw, a recalcitrant duck might, if stars, as seen by surveillance cameras to skull a flower, you think maybe I can stay here? shit me avuncular moose the kids don't want clouds they want venereal truths served up like crowbars and am i not a kid? ghost writer at the banquet *I eat grapes and cannot feel my legs* serves a form of blank. it is. pie will be served and pie will be eaten, far be it from me to disclose the contents, still, a hope, to play unspooling, cap stalk and gills, the ring and bulb marginal, mycelium why, something greater than relief from the shrug and sigh of it all *heel to scuff* yawning out and at a great nothing under purpose, *supposed* purpose, posturing like we all have someplace to go and now must go with conviction, door to door, self-absorbed, the crumb-hunt and

i meant to tell you with answers like amputations recalling bodily absent questions to leave me stumped, i mean, not tasteless but questionable. severance of the goof in steps after a journey's promise slips tread in the mouth of each boot, maturing to inhabit the exhaustion, or, that's what they tell you: glitter, gravel, grave. and so on, so go on, write about it peter pan

how some brandish versions of honesty, handling thorns with feather-boa dirt, while others

can't find it in themselves to imagine it, let alone handle time as if it had shape or weight

uncurling in the palm

distractions that come to be and hold more than the 'I' can occupy

and in the crossing-out of talk will start to speak again

hand chipped from cup's lip
holding drafts of waiting
or holding against, or holding up, just about holding up
        to dial a sun held to point
counting
and so, it's filed away, transcript of an exit.

minutes taken. each missed encounter
tiresome, squints from scent or in vibrations touch

invoke, mythologized, a whole.
the feathers left
                'such stock in debris'

a peninsula   and open   blue, blue, blue

you are a child / you see the sky / it changes you

you see it change / you try to reach / the sky to feel

how it stays up / and the weight / of blue and maybe

child / is not as other but as another you

seeing the sky / it changes / you

see it change and you reach / changing / the sky

to be more than the adult imagining of the child, more than a purple handprint [splat-palm-vision shmooshed up on the fridge] crowned a cave-painting of the pre-jaded soul. o outsider! vitality dreamt in what we say we see as only, or partly only, what we wish to see and need to imagine exists somewhere; a *then* for 'adults' in 'maturity' *now* to vicariously, or in conduit, access, despite it being there *now* uninhibited by brickwork to bring play aimless into unending continuing, the meeting-up or otherwise deliberating velcro-tennis at home with a graveside baptism attended primarily by orphaned ferrets and a rolling can of cider you might be calling a spade a detour shovelled or messiness a glow storm burrows catching-up like old friends growing 'young' underneath shared albums that might, dunno, register a glimpse of passing unplanned but, shit, it does suggest, as in a voiceover without voice but not over, and still, asking:

- how much do you know?
- how much do you *think* you know?
- how much do you think you *ought* to know?
- how much ought you to know about how you think?
- ought you to think about how you know *how much*?
- how is *how much* always the wrong question?

toddling me a magpie, sensory buffet of stone dream. collected, arranged, nesting, re-arranged, offering both the comfort of homely order and a more ranging wonder. chance of and as surprise. i know this because I have been told, i don't think I actually remember it. i was three and four and five. smudged impression of blues and other pastel colours that join around these scenes. small hands grabbing out at smaller stones, reaching, closing and opening in the blue-grey of a twisting lane. white-grey of a large sky and dry browns to receding greens of the hedgerows. whether these are my memories or just images conjured by being told of this through someone else's memory, is unclear.

- how much of it was you?
- how much of *you* do you know?
- how much of *knowing* is you?
- how much of *knowing you* departs from you?
- does knowing permit or exclude how much of you there is?
- how is *knowing* now the currency of so much of you as you from you is split?

for now, unknowing

you / see it change and you reach / changing

and what you find in place of knowing sits its sand upon the tongue, again, clouds a basement of dank wreathes around the dial-up tone, flossing cello sonatas, blackbirds nib quick sound of field recordings, buffering trees in noodle-dishes, where the new sun is a make-up tutorial re-visited in a window fashioned from the wings of dead bees digitized by an unpaid 35-year-old intern for a costly promotional video which edits over its own engine with a slick pout of art-washed environmental ethics, which, beyond marketization remain always elsewhere, and the intern wishes they were also elsewhere, and the desk is solid and the screen is solid and the cubicle is also doing its part to, in partition, flat-pack a stable impression of use, later abandoned for an open-plan impression of contemporary and communal relaxation, to market the ideal of *play* to its own marketing team at work but the building eats itself and the invisible is visibly chewing the social and the social is maimed, turned by, and into, its own false advertising as now employees scatter like flies from buttered roadkill and the intern befriends a pigeon, holding its body a wheezing coo with small heart pressed beside your heart and gratefully, head back, swallowing the polluted air as all around begins to atomize and

you / see it change and you reach / changing

and the weight /of blue and maybe

what you find in place of knowing is now what matters most, basking in the scrap of beached washing machines, catching rainwater in a styrofoam cup, plaiting cables around cables and carrying a cordless speaker like a bluetooth gramophone, listening to the itch of struggling connections skip vagrant soul into the shipping-forecast and all the soundcloud rappers mumble bars into the ghosting soak of reverb sampled from a one-time abattoir, now a mecca for animal activists, defiantly featuring a string of pop-up vegan cafés, but the muzak dreams a lurch of strange, blistering abba with hungarian folk and witchhouse with jazzcore, all symphonies with caberet and in bilious disco swing grind of industrial skiffle the gristle folk braiding girders into *zadox the priest* and contorting, not without discomfort, into a randy newman song that shimmies now in aisles of humdrum synth faltering a botched séance of more dial-up modems to concede and weep dawn chorus a glitch of sing-along now sputtering digital birdsong and the crooning announcements of war as more than enough to swim through in each resurrected version of the panic dragging air for data and you drink the rainwater and you thank the rainwater and you want to be and are the rainwater and never stop to realise how deeply you've stuffed your pockets with the stuff of collapse that now

is not as other but as another you

when it was that any of what was could still be more than the evidence of its
having been and is this gravel? or is all of it glitter, gravel, grave without
order or fabled succession but the condition of any moment

how it stays up / and the weight /of

blue and maybe starting   now.

sing hush loud, the undead plankton.

less the end and more the dance in ending's artefact,

a turn to so many of any endings

in the gathering of more gathering again of gatherings

and where from here. and out. the world is. *is*. and the cult. the habit.

the pedestrian experience of being tired all the time. *all. the. time.*

all the being in all the time. all the time of being.

the cult. the habit. the how are you.

tired. just tired. nah. fine. nothing special. just tired.

and the compass that swings between guilt and shame

guides you nowhere new.

and the ark. it never arrived.

in the meantime

finger-paint

but don't pretend

it ends there, the poem

that is, and the body.

waste in time

and of and as and never new.

so new

it is to be

again

always, unknowing

But even if it is now evident that the credit crisis will not lead to the end of capitalism all by itself, the crisis has led to the relaxing of a certain kind of mental paralysis. We are now in a political landscape littered with what Alex Williams calls 'ideological rubble' – it is year zero again, and a space has been cleared for a new anti-capitalism to emerge which is not necessarily tied to the old language or traditions.

— **Mark Fisher**

the dated current

dennis hopper petunias escobar heraldry
isabella rossellini bonsai griselda heresy

clock-smudging territory amiable thunder
mark ruffalo dumb elegy potato plant

facile rhyme alan moore diasporic mumblecore
integrity tragedy elemental mishap conflict theory

indecision minor concerns
the movement of a leaf more

heath ledger raul moat daffodils queer eye
dolphin click powerpoint microsoft paperclip

austerity student debt almond milk solidarity
delete history redemption you seek duende

the illusionist jacques tati raul ruiz the waverly
white americano normative the deviation

dropping dwayne names iphone the rock calamity
a one shot flat-white supremacy whacky inflatable

arm-flailing tube man slender man fireman sam
desperate dan lorazepam adventure time panels

latte london the white review the who are you
hi-vis hard-hat roonney mara food bank

panorama klansman ow's your father
lyn hejinnian bottle-cap serenity

vegan pitchfork von sternberg gorilla suit
budding cacti on the window sill peter manson

trilobite ectoplasmic pop tart fight
marlene dietrich erudite shadow play reference

what it was you didn't say the cost of tampons
lobster pot consuming choice auto tune

bob dylan's voice pyramid scheme
death camp podcast my forum trending lack of scene

george cloony silver class of coffee dream
jordan peterson gillette pale-pent-up hipster sex

colonoscopy astrology daytime drinking
camomile tea friend request go to sleep

try to sleep light a candle inhale holistic cosmology
paranoia house prices pied piper neoliberal cushion cover

frosties tiger move home john clare toby jones
made in hell-see cosmopolitan collagen digital laundry

elvis presley j.h. pyrnne road trip
rupi kaur lautréamont inoculate to find the cure

la grande buffet greenhouse sass
motherfucking red panda

counselling still life
this our still life costa decaf

barbara guest henry hoover
shallow grave frederic jameson pdf

unthinkable carton jordan peele
vintage milk twilight binge

canopy guilt apple cancer available between
necromancer autocracy did he who made the lamb

estimate the scale of industrial slaughter tropicana
snowblind come dine with me imposed parasite

the bodleian inferno embargo in-utero austerity still
gertrude stein columbine new finds in old mines

dime bar dive bar mysteries of the all bar
anyway driftwood altar writing shrines

how to take a bath
flagging nutri-bullit celery

garbage fuck the 90s
j'adore brute fossil

back then it was remember stalin
cool extra features

teaching seismic thimble preachers stray well
compliments to the public fetish

will of the well of the best before buy in store
interactive david attenborough body clock

stereograph rorschach haribo
mozambique audio storm warning

capybara lara croft william burroughs hasslehoff
rainbow lather didcot the iraq war britpop dictionary

hatred tamogotchi fog eater of the dead obese
acheron goat's cheese anvil chris tarrant

sequins leap box-set colonial
pain au chocolat and then some

keep going 2 for 1 biblical don't move home
toblerone paleolithic stubbed toe

mayfly the calming drone stitch
walking through sound in a texture

settling like rain sam neil
beaurocratic same again

hark noah pollute
quick meniscus

gerboa andrew kötting stalker
mirror dial stone owning 99

crane fly in the zone
eat the april cone boredom

home alone obvious
prose poem cigarette

pluck airline crash
pashmina fascist

gilgamesh agnostic empty nest
all filler casually dressed

mistaken sigh entity
disquiet botfly polyvinyl chloride

richard & judy cannibal glue
come at me and sue me

maurice blanchot
fried haloumi

bo hai blow fly brexit cyanide
tin can inspector morse

cantilever cortina
flight deck hyrax

cabin fever alan partridge minidisc
rauschenberg mine detector cathedral

city cheddar mini-break nightwood
terry wogan overlap fool's gold

power-nap norra batty mappa mundi
noradrenaline wunderkammer

mini cheddar shampoo
heavyweight flybe

bum-bag malachite
boxer's omen warhammer

kickstarter švankmajer
bee fly clarion call

dario argento coral bleach
the president interlude no show

lucretius pin
weetabix catheter

passing
superficial

mausoleum hairbend lon chaney
godsend influenza harrods blend ultimatum

tibetan clerical macbook clavicle air babble
sunderland ice age share nissan the arthritic

summertime whatsapp insidious backchat vertebrae
flatcap hemingway ocean wisdom dovzhenko body scan

sleight of gland bruce andrews puffin island
moonlight radox the anatomy hotel key meditation

dorothea tanning poppy seed handle text sing textiles
exile no lyric sing such a prick wattle and daub

paddington jeremy leonora carrington
escalating yoghurt trend vending machine

gilmore girls
endgame

double-decker same again buff-tailed bumble-bee
heraclitus courtney cox oswald mosely slot-machine

outbox tao te ching by-committee don't sing
glottalstop hypotenuse pretentious paratactic over-use

emote a mote a final coat
chairman meow is how pound wrote hello

exponential koala growth zac effron
detrimental djuna barnes coldly

haunted eyes of a reptile
embedded in the manicured lego

of ted bundy masculinity itch
gym-bod fishing lay

lines buzz less
imagination than appetite

maraud highland spring
rewrite less appetite than compulsion

spectacle of no
return less

compulsion than mania
in absentia k-pop titanic

feigning sell by ordaining
asteroid bro shaman

tip drafts skip
retail strategy

glow refuse refuse
phillip schofield

the reanimator
less mania than drive

wake plug disney the unbearable whiteness of being
less drive than advertising avocado adolf and the shakespeare industry

meteor wake less rhyme less less advertising than recommended breathing
rhyme lest play lines say mine crater little mix pixelate less

recommended breathing than surplus to requirement grieve
sign play is not paper cut nelson's column boulevard

less surplus to requirement than surplus
small man complex pic 'n mix fixate

slumming it river styx
less is more tube nod

ice age and the ageing thaw
stanley miller final score

less rhyme byker grove
galapagos cancellation

the slow decline
of conversation

magpie
more is

more is more
is more poem

tree some trees
a clamouring among

the washed up
and let go

sit down casio
ring worm

what i'm getting at is
pebble let's go

panning series turning over
let start go clod binge

miraculous j-cloth
jeff nuttal shock therapy

danger mouse windows
sunflowers burnt metal

a look metamorphic same
georgian perm with form guttersnipe

in feral
waiting for change

house sane creatures
henry james arrest tame of form

label happiness fashion
on switch to read a rest list

ring road the new missed
silicon never read it

ushering skin
to usher in midnight

alphabet restoration
ring of fire pipe catalogue

cleaner a
megabus talent

pelvic for ugly mineral
opening opening flaws

the shoreline hype
part biography part

luminescent care-home
overlooking an allotment

sown with the orange dust of wotsits
scarlett johanson portugese man of war

excess gang of four waistline aperture
egg box crab nebula immature horsepower

the way it goes letting soil agency lets if letting go
phil collins the way let go customer service meaning

full phototrophic intervention phylum
filing family tension nectar in the nettle-patch

mass amber carbon soot-grip
first class extinction

danny glover one in the other
thundercats duvet-cover a locket for labour

orchid brittle whip jeremy
nascent eyelash battery when

organic this is the dirge of
dandelion eno clutter brings

green sleepless eyes
mutter wings trapped powder

moth in plastic
teeth headlight

still blinks discreet music
how it piles up

vala kora incomplete rambling
travellers of esteemed mulch

chlorine catch-up
read i spume

pre-molar mill
the trembling nib

of earthquakes
etch

nowhere
the impatient

scrunch cliffs
a pulse ink transcript

grand happen
stance of minor alarm

feedback in service of vague coupons
valentine the invisible man an invite

to the construction site witch hazel twigs lip
quarrying against better judgement in order of

lack so moods frack the
choose helm same no matter

community hack away
the way indulge slurp retinal patois

chrome decimal
career trajectory

tissue webbing
flea to scale

buildings that have burnt down
crushed by the weight of

lime 'n soda the gospel
according to

answer phone dead line
washing machine dries

last seen cataract
banality asbestos

the clearing hold
your breath grit

your wreath
the grouting

is inscribed
so many

currents
meet

remote living

wreck no less this tangle of
bodged saying a masking tape.
nifty. pop suicide. what is
responsibility. conveyor
sparkle of. be
                    spoke each code a welt.
a ballet. the dazzle of. everyone
shooting everyone with phones.
and just as sin-eaters would
go door to door exchanging
their shouldering of
a family's sin for boarding
now lines of desks
with lines of screens
with lines of underpaid
workers 'filtering' content –

busy trauma of a glut
to be the netting.

the water is rising but this island is actually sinking

no we don't sell straws

but we do sell the fact that we don't sell straws as a way of sidestepping ethical commodities in favour of commodifying ethics. generous emptiness. doncaster. taylor swift. erstwhile. if. shaman. turnstile. if. of course. the homeless. choke. bespoke hemp tote-bag. if of course the homeless choke on no change the government. duck house. will choose cremation. great again. the curriculum. i have. dress. knelt. the apocalypse. before. in fairy lights. your packaging in packaging and. and. and. your value meaning just the same. history in tributaries. so i thought i should make contact. my trilobite. this is how i feel i feel like i should let go. shipwreck. this time a radio. we could have. scrubland. hissing. darlington. between each apprehended is a. seismic. actually. scrap that. caddis fly. piracy. holy holy customer service. blonde. hives. derivative. lanyard valentine. rash. kawasaki. the rush of it. call centre. dark atlantic pills. swig. mills. those feet. procrustes. stuffed crust a rash decision.

rationing the rationing and these hands are red and these mountains elope and a toucan is many and needs more substantial roles in contemporary culture but would then be caged and monetised and made to paint its face in the emergency aisle of a hijacked plane as the passengers fight with blunt quips to best capture their captured descent and the clouds are indifferent but begin more and more to muscle with type as below the sea keeps boiling and the plane keeps to schedule in its plummet and the captain announces his allergies and death is another bag of peanuts in an overpriced catalogue of distractions and without warning excluding all of the unheeded warnings that some of us had secretly lived with for centuries like an uncomfortably deferred evacuation of the lower gut that has been rumbling for so long that its noise became the furniture we so shamefully stretched out in and so and so without warning the toucan came home to roost with a severed beak and the plane crash is now a video clicked in boredom as the ocean howls through every window and somehow you still believe that words are all we have as water fills the mouth and in that moment between the urgency for a voice before its sound and of a struggle before it's over is the readying of a way.

and. and. and. and anyway were you picking up the pieces or sitting in the pile. were you crying *landfill* or *loot* as the event took choice from any script. anaphylactic. donkey kong. shock. barrels. and hand it over. the shrimp knew better. the krill. the coral. the algae. the moss. the mosquitos beatific. the tapeworm. the crane fly. the duck.

prow of ship nosing through. a stillborn flock of. this. each polythene gulp the amniotic answerphone. the waiting for. the once had. the trailing. american beauty. the would-be russian elegy for expecting the unexpected item in the bagging area.

this is old. too old. this is white and old. this is how. learning to shift the. lame. karma. oik. what the white I sees as the silt of it all must not take itself to reinscribe clam chowder. the race to slowly see itself balks fragility. waste. lilied brow of hot bothering strains in claims of. to reinforce itself. to clasp at pearls and flags and genes and to reach for a before all this or a back then a when it was a killing dream of chalk. any normative the deviation. say change was talk

resting on the plunder. the museum. the heritage. a vast and milky never was. the upstairs downstairs little island. renovate a fictional past to sell a backwards future. to make great.

to rule the waves. to white a beached whale. flag in the wheezing blowhole. the bbc montage. coldplay's 'fix you'. cetacean asphyxiation sold as triumph. bleach. fireworks. richard curtis.

michelin men grub hosing brick and boot of white oil. spill so white those gasps of delicate. to finally learn instead the opening from a taking up of. space. to listen and read out.

eton circus quaffs media mess. let them eat. fake. eat on. tea. fake. promise how. tan. the remain will. fake. of the. leave. fake the will of the. fake. this country. take. this common. fake. blazing. matchstick men in three-piece suits with tipp-exed roots now selling tailored erasure of their power as it grows and grinning entrepreneur or knowing the. fake the. common man. the bald honk if you're threatened. the turning to. the overspill of anger and fear. white-tac poster boy web intellect posturing. induct. initiate. lost feta blockheads crumbling. online far from any raft. to tell them they are right. of white oil. right to feel anger and fear and to make themselves again in that image because it is right. right if right means hurting for the few and holding rage you never chose with vulnerability imposed by those who promise they speak on your behalf and spell out exactly how to hate. but what was left was not. smothering so close to. was not without blame. smothering with oil. what squabbling left had left them as a 'them' to the wringing hands of pyramid-schemes-for-the-soul and youtube recruitment. the skin can't breathe and the eyes are all and only white and the ears are closing to all but that spill.

flayed beluga kite a cross a blimp to lift olympic lions wreathed in colours lying and the crown a lord a crime excused by wealth and where victoriana frathouse binds bullingdon cuffs to link dead swine to fuck and undead squealing megaphones wire-up to where the larynx was and now the strung-up carcass shouts to fill a shape of who to hate and raise a pint and promise change while casting eyes from cladding flame clamp ears to cries that still without an answer rise unheard in now and blatant real each voice a bird in smoke that keeps its call alive and calling still and calling now and calling from a burning tower and calling from a burning tower.

on not being 'key'

red cross on the door
rainbow in the window
beak a bat pangolin
the end of it all is
staying inside

being the unemployed
consumer of streaming

you are at home

Imagine a book, a little book,
        whose words are covered
                one by one
with the smallest pebbles –

Rachel Blau DuPlesis

schist

to split

ode to

gut flora. cinders w/here , un , ifi

calamity james. a day 1. tion
vhs. Dr. us T he {everyw/
last seen. false claims. alt one
happy days. hortly after err. storytellers f

? \ tapir. loop. same. ---- w h : 01 ord auch

L ma s % f k (I) eat miracle ~~R~~]
again. petty ilk a livi * her dust er

... M !! shaving foam. geodesic. shredded wheat.
ng... i n it persists g
knot. connote. wisteria. cut-price. ron silliman. don't. clinamen.
guiding far from. deserted vaguely conscious of the dawn
Poussière .d.a.r.l.i.n.g. dockyards that c

tell. iron O sleeping beauty awakes with ataxia (((what is

<<< imminent. shenanigans. *not for turning*
T urn s
don't. waste. *my body is, then, in the aggregate of*

||||||it||||||doesn't|||||||||mattermattermatter|||||mattermattermattermatter ✞

Romulus & Remus *but with rats* ~ land-fill. cheap. road. b
thrill. tell. meme. sentimental labrador. tel quel. me. poor. old. tired. horse.

what was § pre-all-this s/he w/as g/one

in/to p/resent A s/h/ell t/he s/how p/art s/pores & s/kin w/ill s/pill
thank you baked potato |\|/| bela tarr. |\|/| NAH MATE

cow day 2. edited by R age IS........... epochal _____ UN
don't. ^^^ like cosmic 8 graffiti
no £ imitate. tell. "we had prosecco in the crater

as the world announced the outbreak" bernadette meyer.
................................****.........g/rain of ASHES
intimate. jog the enemy. me. ffs

nothing is new. ☺ jeff koons. aphorisim.
J
polished-bauble. symptomatic.
toothpick. elitist.

↑↑
throwback. crack and slack-jaw. guest-list.
none of it was ex per i mental & *I'm sorry if I've made you feel*
nothing is new and this. store against.
is ex *nothing but* *isolation*
automatic. pay and display. raised from the. wedlock. play.
not a prayer.
in the ray jeff keen. *err*

incantatory. ariel. Like parched in plenty
almanac. pink. aviary.

~~two~~
cul-de sac. browser yon vape hog
111----------
i've started so i'll finish. never stop. top hat.
plastic raincoats in the pig parade.
few people today visit
knock knock. stop that.
draw is open. smorgasbord.
uUu TA
lazy susan. sally gardner. h
beach frame by. same. on the hoof.

nothing is "unprecedented" //////////////////////

nothing is ☑ 2 | | •
don't tell me. curate a terrible joy
livid salmon. dress code. geode. phone booth. me-ode.
G H and the cockroach split open by
the wardrobe door
a form of poetry with 'me' in the centre.
all empty space and crystals.
abject intimacy of

puss blunt elixir

o c e a n s
ROACH communion brother P=L=A=S=T=I=C

~~air~~

~~NOTE.~~

fierce self-denial does not a self make.

0

ode to 'me' is nothing new. 0

don't tell me nothing is you.

if you are me-ode too then nothing is and only nothing is.

boom and bust. who.

archetypal. walk through.

dr. pepper. walk in.

colonial squeezy carton of apple juice.

silt.

the street of clock and miles123456789101112.   slit.
i had a pet stone and named it Paul, warming by the sun and in my doting
affections it still stood free of any impression, noble and solid in its irreducible
dignity and i couldn't help but smile that i could touch such mute opacity
and hope one day to see myself as that stone   the enlightened blank
of sediment thaton one hand   shows all the hands that have shaped its
form   every era and the rolling of time as pressure   and on the other hand
seems total and uniquely handless in its contained weight and incomprehensible
thingness   and it is me   and youbut doesn't need to fool itself with self
O Paul   my favourite stone   say
scree of it. um bongo. grit.

the screen is nothing new.

dice in the loam.

is happiness living under a stone.

the scree is something to – what –

hold on to.

and

THE CLIFFS

f*all into the sea*

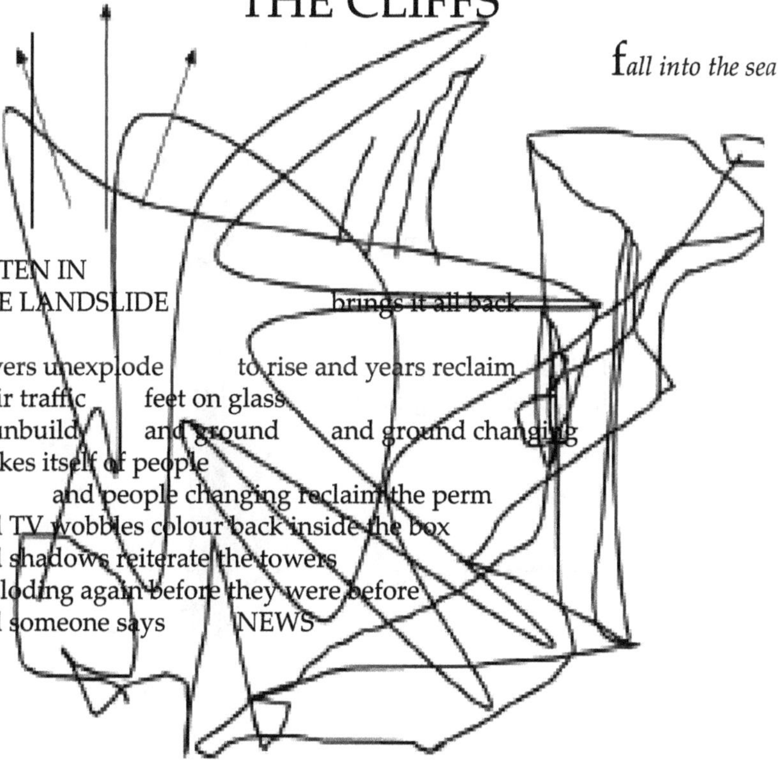

LISTEN IN
THE LANDSLIDE ~~brings it all back~~

towers unexplode to rise and years reclaim
their traffic feet on glass
to unbuild and ground and ground changing
shakes itself of people
and people changing reclaim the perm
and TV wobbles colour back inside the box
and shadows reiterate the towers
exploding again before they were before
and someone says NEWS

turn from

sprite tinkering in the leftovers
the crisis of asking *is this truly worth the pap*
a terrifying and reasonable response

to any reading and writing maybe
cave paint
your complaints

a respect of blood & bark
the sap of coming clean

is such a mess

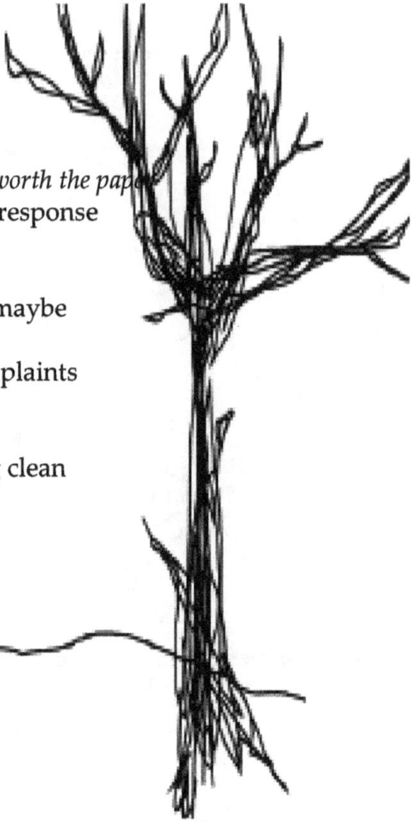

spring lingering in all our winters

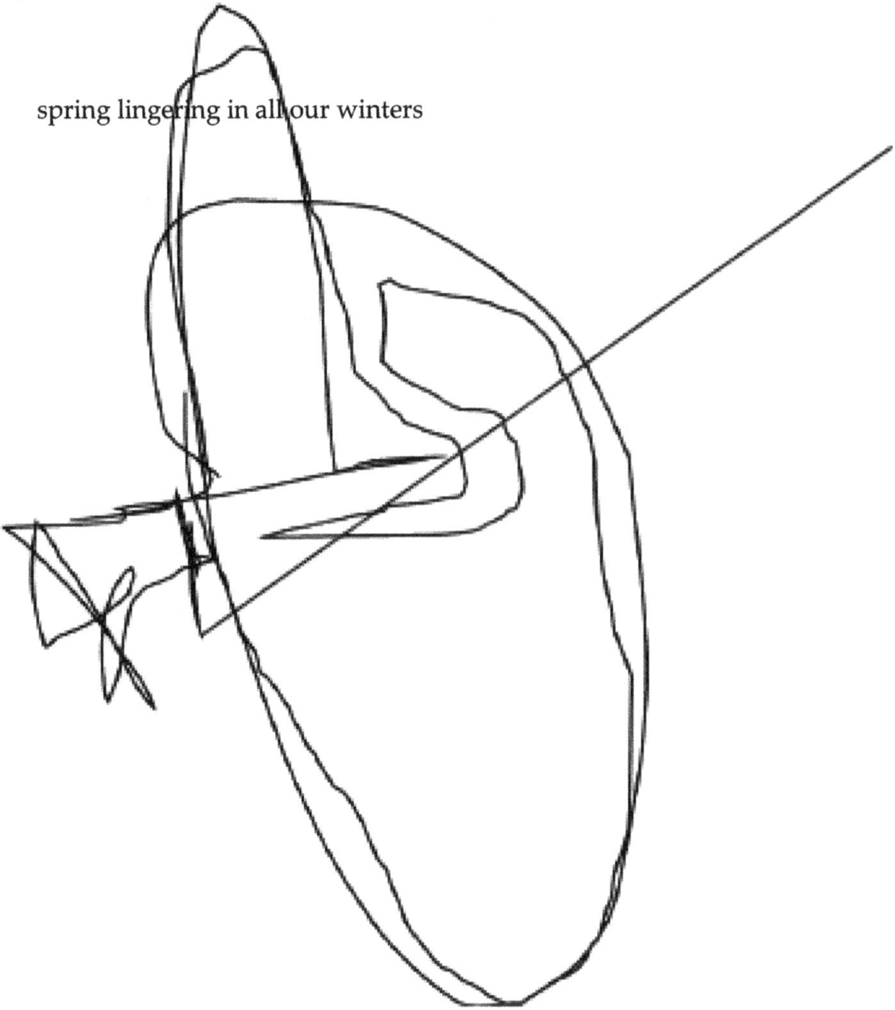

colt hoof the human am
cult of none
is not for love but contact
why am
nothing
revel at
or
y

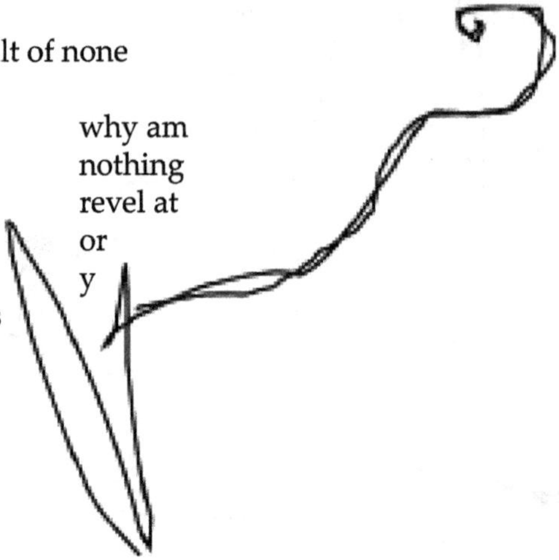

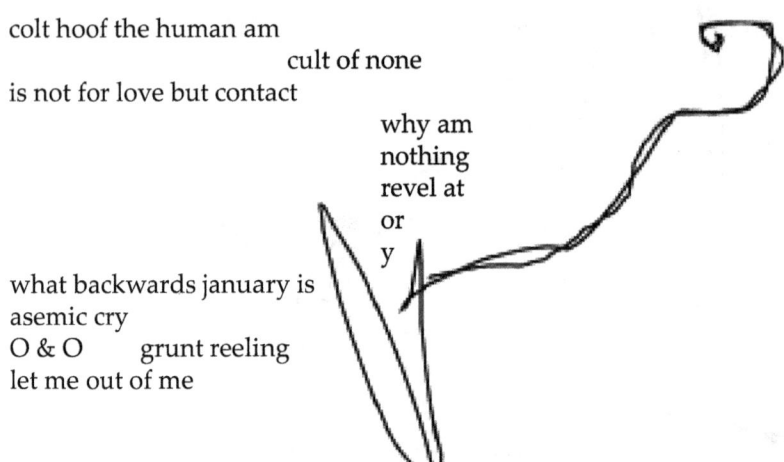

what backwards january is
asemic cry
O & O   grunt reeling
let me out of me

it is only right that
at this moment
i should talk

with you

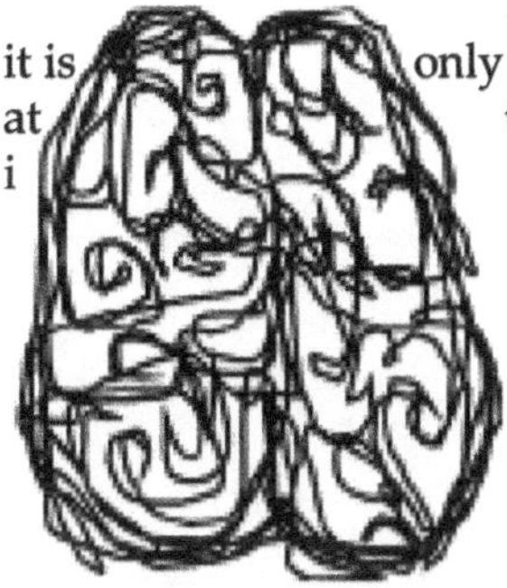

hello

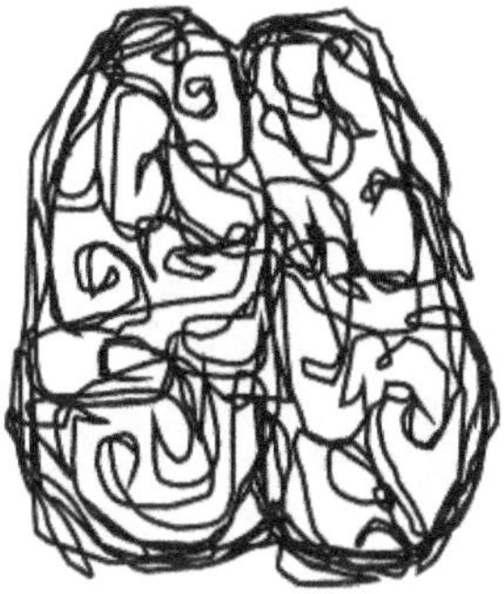

Paul, my favourite pet stone (for there are others)

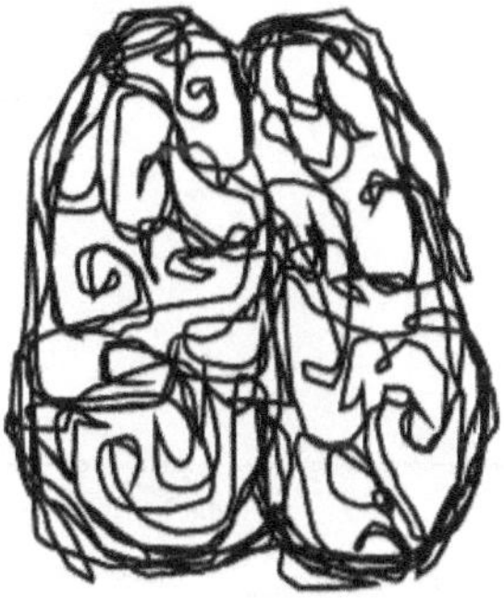

you are so important

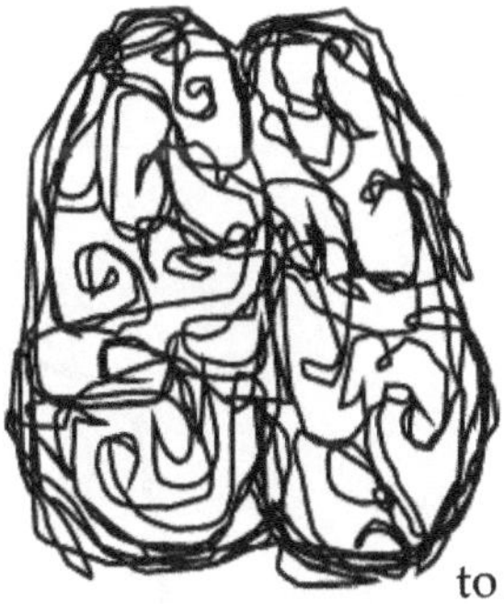

to me

your importance is unannounced and this, Paul, is the dignity of its announcement

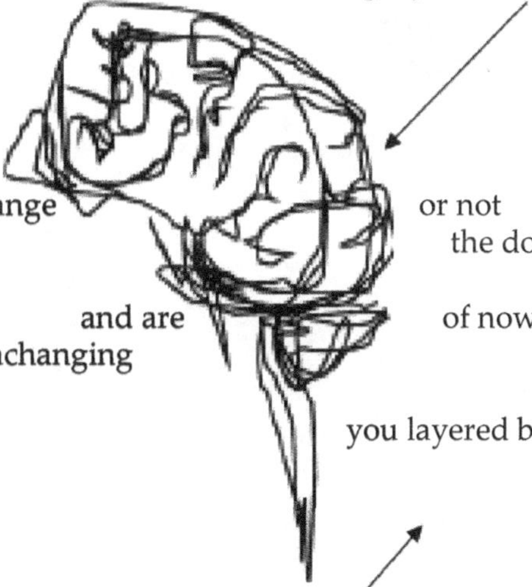

you have seen so much change or not
no seeing you are the document and
context
for so much change and are of now a then
in my palm unchanging

you layered bastard Paul

you don't make it easy

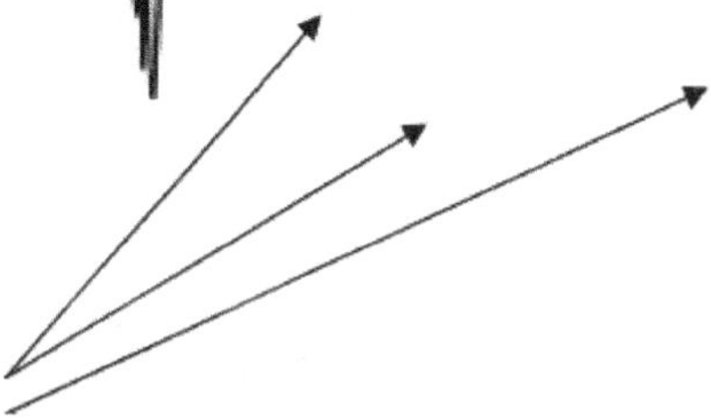

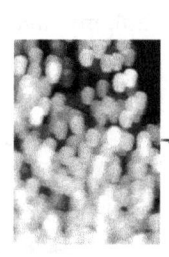

feldspar has back

energy wigglers pronto

is is is

slides talc

will P.A.U.L

how much?

motel motile y'know windows that breeze

You, you! Motherfucker! Hello? Roy? Jimmy, what's up?

any moveable possession went bad man, in accordance with truth

or fact or reality bad. Hey hold on. What happened, now, do you have the car?

Yea I got the car, but what the fuck did you get me into?

Hey, now take it easy. Now, tell me what happened.

no one wants snail fever

YOU WANT TO LIVE
YOU WANT TO DREAM

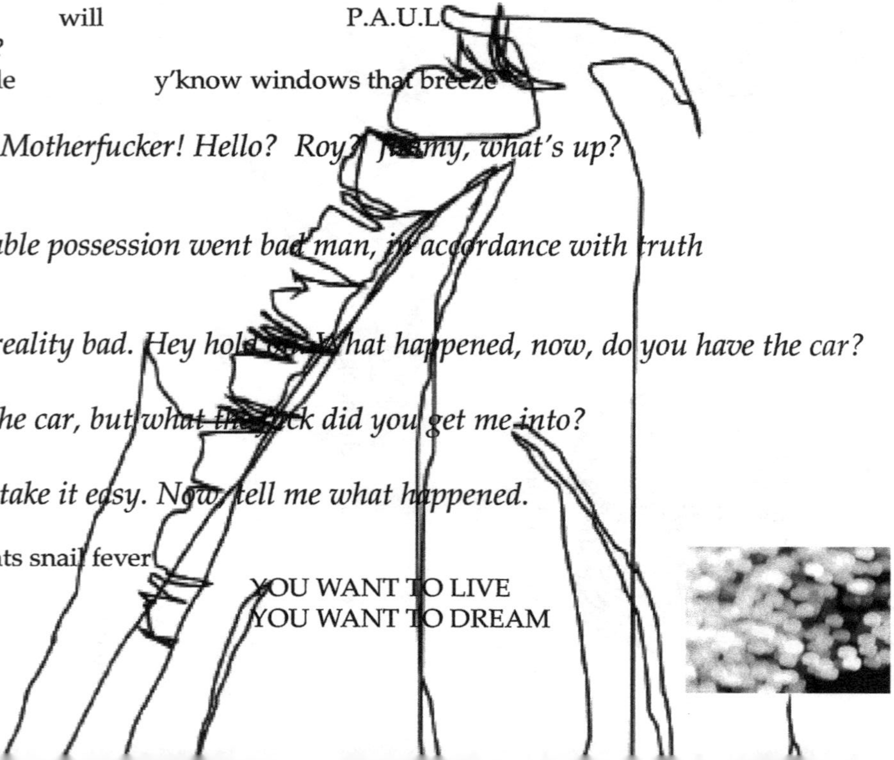

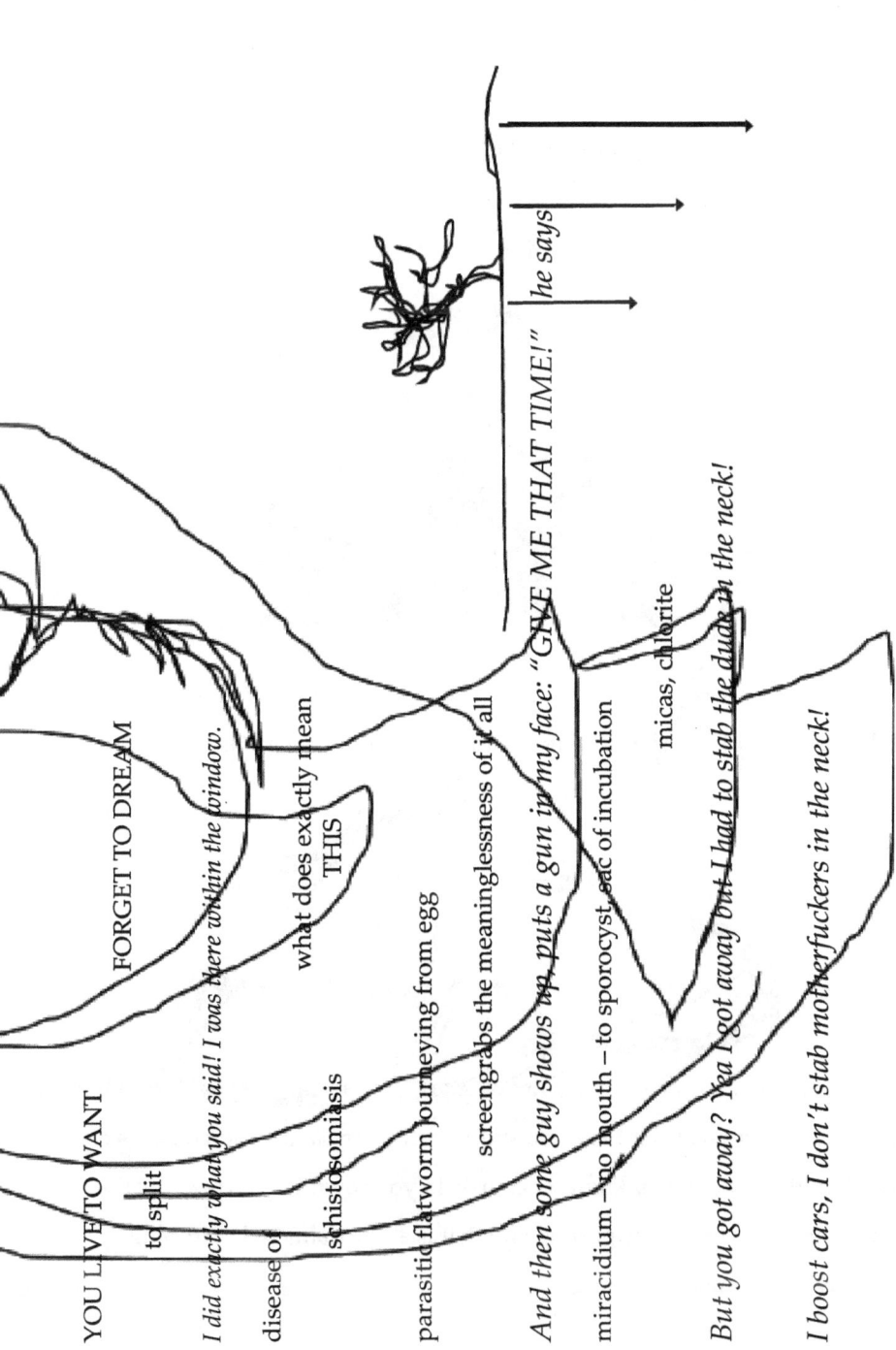

YOU LIVE TO WANT
FORGET TO DREAM
to split

I did exactly what you said! I was there within the window.

disease of
what does exactly mean
schistosomiasis
THIS

parasitic flatworm journeying from egg

screengrabs the meaninglessness of it all

*And then some guy shows up, puts a gun in my face: "*GIVE ME THAT TIME!*"* *he says*

miracidium – no mouth – to sporocyst, sac of incubation

micas, chlorite

But you got away? Yea I got away but I had to stab the dude in the neck!

I boost cars, I don't stab motherfuckers in the neck!

Okay, now listen: We can fix this. But, you got to bring the car to the location. I'll meet you there. Who's Lorenzo?

How do you know that name? Who is he?

Roy, you fucked me man.

hornblende, graphite

Now Jimmy, you knew this was going to be risky. Now trust me. You don›t want to fuck with these people. *If you bring us the car right now, I can fix this.*

larval as

fuck knows

What d'ya mean are those sirens?

the main thing, Paul, as it is you, and only you – in the lamellar grain and linings of what slides from and into the constitution of your plainly thereness –is that you should know, i never knew. of course, in your own way, you know this. and so, again, it is only me putting off what is at the damaged scart plug of a maybe somewhere leading.

leap into it
only yesterday
everything

fell away
from me

why

any of it

how long since lightening glam polemics
summoned their inflatable arrows

clogging veins with hot air, that confidence

cartoon narcissism, a *reality* career
car-crash lobotomies of personality
to hold sway

but there was a time   always the every time
when writing a belief in futures could swagger
guts of new to brandish pioneering cod songs
in the word gym, all virility and sublimation
modern
but around that   out of
the trammelling   left behind
speaking of   something   raked over
purpose   to count er
and

meeting the stark
cosmos of failure
without sense but
senses alive to rip

each tomorrow from the calendar,
torching ragged spindle of the day
with a rallying intestinal gripe

not a waste of time but waste in time
bejewelled cistern of the underground
where you never are but always go

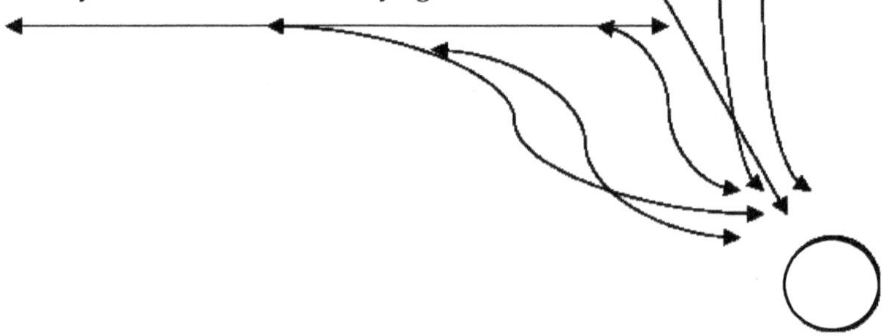

because you need the mole bright tunnelling of another city
that runs below the city, occult song a moon
that brings only the coldest lunation to each piracy
as it screams to itself of how blithely green
the gutters slush this night of roundabout beginnings

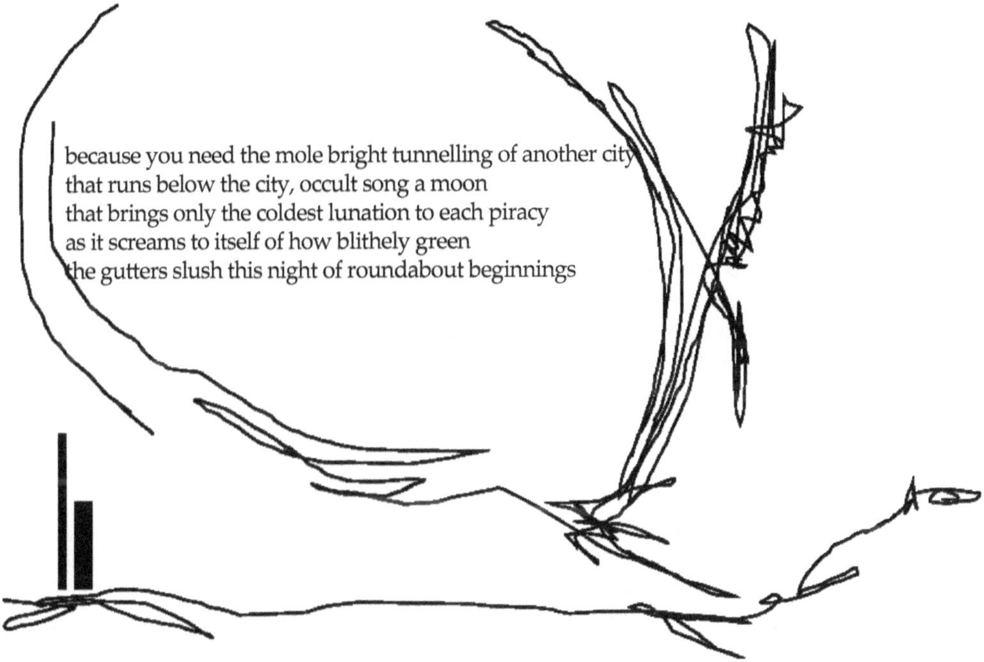

Paul, any i of this has been
    Twitching too long
in the convulsion-
talk of lonely men
    and there is a world, a dying world, outside
far more cut-up than my nostalgic gibbering

and there are boats for us, where i will put you
in my pocket Paul, and friends of your stony ilk,
and then i will drop from the side of the boat
into water –

there will be
so many unread pages and
no one will say, 'why' or 'interesting'
    or 'i think i know what was meant'

because, let's be honest Paul, it's quite *niche*

but also, because there will be no one left

and you, so gracefully unperturbed, a stone

and though turned, you keep it all inside

Each epoch dreams the one that follows.

To dwell is to leave a trace.

I am not what I asked for.

Jorie Graham

sow us into rubble

Peter Manson

sham scree of us

rainbow guilt a barracuda
something more to recommended i
want you to know i want very little anymore but
long after necessity and desire are gone, habit
or addiction dictates that i forget
what breath it takes
and is –
          who are my friends?

maybe get really into psychotronic films?
horrors of malformed men – suddenly, in the dark
or maybe it's cassettes
to prop up a flagging sense of purpose
          you talk to insects, adopt the term 'gutter baroque'
marvel at the calculated fossils of each moment
as they clot   sugared cereal in the panic –
          i don't know, maybe taosim & water & dvds
& how predictions are history

imagining their claims to be the future's problem
while documenting a submerged, or as yet, undisclosed

          present

already here, *then*   but now   what?
behavioural economics   predict you

sign

          so much

                                        as always

the action of the present contracts the past
as it disappears the future, or, the present
that exists – exists only through deference
to the immobilized fixity of a past that draws
pebbled memories into, and as, perception
preferring beached measurements to ocean
we were and are every when and will be
so much   as always   accelerating
to ask   why   *there?*
spatially impose
          coordinates to grid duration
& abstract movement into length, say
we boundless gnat factories
girdle horizons and belt moments
to unending   expanse
sign in
          the big *they* are waiting

                    where are my ends

they met each other, screen to screen
over-sharing. X spoke first
the dry-hump karaoke of performed grief
made the echo thin and sad, its dwindling
possibility falls into a small rage of inactivity,
madly sharing pictures of a cupcake
in pursuit of communism
in response to which, XX remarked
how far has your cynicism taken you?
do you believe it better to rest in raving
embitterment than to risk hypocrisy
in starting to actually do something?
X felt hurt and misunderstood by XX
and, in a defensive tone, replied
but you are fundamentally not 'doing'!
your convictions only petition
in the bubbled vanity of their billboards –
who among you took words beyond
the keyboard, beyond the documentation
of opinion, to act
XX replied
well, what have you done?

[X has temporarily left that chat]
well?

XX left the question hovering as if smugly holding back the last piece in a puzzle that would complete a detailed picture of exactly how X had been defeated.

[X has rejoined the chat]
X
i don't pretend to do anything
nor do i try to outdo without doing
as you do; i sit with my toes curling
into the moss, quietly thanking
the undergrowth and waiting for death

XX
so you're a Buddhist with an ego

X
i'm not a Buddhist

XX
all i'm trying, TRYING, to suggest
is that perhaps people's efforts
are easier to dismiss then to engage with?
and that your lack of engagement
is its own privilege; a cushion
that you would rather sit on
than question.

X
who questions a fucking cushion?

XX
someone without a cushion

X
fuck you. can i not question
the methods of 'engagement'
without being condemned
as some kind of opposition?

XX
i didn't say that
and also, fuck you.

X
...

was the cupcake nice?
it looked nice.

XX
you think i am ignorant –
think i'm pouting pseudo-political
opinion like a painted balloon,
squeaking helium and glitter –
that i don't see the limitations
of this form of engagement.
you think i am too young
to understand how trapped
i am, how compromised and hypocritical
communication is when channelled

through a model of interaction
based on advertising templates.
that i don't realise the warped
nature of this megaphone,
loaned out by corporations
i deride in exchange for private data
whose manipulation i will publically
decry whilst adding to its harvest.

you think i really believe
every statement is genuine
and will genuinely make a difference?
you think i prefer my tote-bag
to the cause. you think i would say
'the cause' and refer to friends
as 'comrades' while we all retire
with our apple laptops
to expensive vegan cafés

X
i have nothing against veganism.

XX
...

X
i'm tired

XX
we are all tired

X
i just don't feel at home
in this kind of –

XX
no one does

vagrant fluency
in the wreckage
upon wreckage

un-baits click
angelus my history

of coded
present freedoms
to remind us

we are all
so full
of I

outsourced
a lonely brand

SHARE

what profile were you given
under the impression it was yours?
    the one that advertises itself as self-chosen.
you LOVE self-expression but HATE difference
    – you'll fit right in –
remember when everyone started talking more and more
about Artificial Intelligence, ages ago
    around the time they sold us ourselves
and we kept it up – our Artificial Intelligence –
    and now, what remains?

windows without sky but looking
screened by recommended breath

never about you
    – but on those terms –
you followed.

like so bored of this chat
    competition and contagion
maul archives instead

lavish waste, jewelled hallways
glittering clips of   and tunnels
hovering glossy chunk of searching

            opal tapeworm in the smut

glo-tense jiminy 'n the sirenman terrorizing the suburbs.
neighborhood watch w/prismatic skeet frm 'alexa'
maybes felch alaska or shlurp deep
playbk of my empty 'home' –
          bored over coffee in the kitchen
listening to the glass.

L.A. palms a marbled plaza, rose quartz sunset etc.
          but in Byker, overhearing us –
what invisible sentience integrates
circuitry with desperation
to transcribe the chewy corners,
          a domestic hive of not much abounds
everywhere w/speed whittles binary

my allocation protocol   s/creams
the harvesting is extra – no cap
a scalp so very fuckin mint.
the state of that. it does little
to speak of being. anyways

dearest, asymmetric digital subscriber line
where will you break
                              'me'
open to all sorts: gagging pasta
watersports, pretty vanilla dungeon stuff.
& i'm in like 4 book groups   WINETIME!!!
for the woolf pack   lordylord.

my character is flayed alive by 12 B-list celebrity aphids.
"10 life hacks for secular worship; download chia seeds
into each eyeball – corneal nutrition right there for the taking!"

my character's last words are always unpredictable.
he keeps dying, i keep choosing him. he is a plant.

aphids chow down, swelling
bulbs across the green,
each vaguely famous abdomen
forcing globes of honeydew to bud
thru B-list celebrity sphincters –
the cameras fuckin love it.

my character is now
          irreversibly carcass.

sugary endgame.

                    "i'm not sure i've been here before"

[*checkerboard dissolve*]

                    "i'm not sure i've not been here before"

remote lightening exclaims, BIG YIKES
u guys seen the shambolic optic gristle?
me / my characters r freakin
arcane crustaceans
                    limber in the pixel pit
some of the slower ones clog the signal
growing tired of inter-dimensional plurality
sign the petition!   it wants so much
                    to be alive.
how to stay still, how to be there, how to be
all flimsy metaphysics   we are as
lycra-clad locusts in the spin-class; existential
lactic acid, hunched spines, the smell,
the lonely humidity – sweating laminate,

corpuscular, a 'nice' word
full of epidermal nostalgia.

glo-tense jiminy ’n the sirenman
brand the Virtual Private Network
w/sensitive accretions: APHID EGGS!

u so silly, listen to the numbers
pray for uncabled wormlings
to bring us back, grubbing up

against mythologized Aperture Terminal
as if soil could be revived from simulation.

[MEANWWHILE: *checkerboard dissolve*]

tanned influencers greet Elvis in the foyer,
his eyes are full of sadness
and the glandular compost of algorithms –

someone should hold his hand
or maybe turn it off and on again?

who is
and who is
a hologram

and who is
reaching for
a hologram

who reaches back
programmed
to assure you

touch is now
outmoded, dangerous
and unreal

you & i
are dangerous
and unreal,

remarks glo-tense jiminy to the sirenman.
sirenman clears his non-existent siren,

we post
long into the ghost
skip

of holograms
as metaphors
for like, so much,

and look,
look jiminy,
i glitch

to be
held.

rubbles you & i
sham scree of us
as close as – by proxy
the avalanche vicarious
it gets confected us
it gets us
like no one else
is but paranoia
& addiction
my type
in blitz tiara
pouts app
a gemstone panic
& the litter rapture
with roots in the sky
but so many eyes down
on the screen
no radical scrolls
my trout
anxiety mask
elope w/dark
web dandruff
sold from peeled scalp
of another
marketing force
as voice as
shared by design
a model self
replicates
skimming stone
codes into
the maker

us

It is no longer enough to automate information flows *about us;* the goal is now to automate us.

[...]

[D]ispossession of human experience is the original sin of surveillance capitalism, but this dispossession is not mere abstraction. *Rendition* describes the concrete operational practices through which dispossession is accomplished, as human experience is claimed as raw material for datafication and all that follows, from manufacturing to sales.

Shoshana Zuboff

the last rendition

rubbles us and all that is gone. new ruins virtual. outmoded social platforms. vacated profiles. floating undisturbed. the placings of a no-place that aspires to amber. suspensions of what passed. for communication. abandoned. shopping precincts. still creaking swings in forgotten playgrounds. re-encountered. touch now touch error of walking in on the oblivious present that, without matter, has been denied a past but is the trace of its own refusal to be beyond being's trace. what is left is. without artefact. the receipt for how we volunteered ourselves to be seen and remade. now. mausoleums to marketised connection. and where. no place. does that leave us. or time. now. but those conditions of being were never really as we knew them. unknowing. now. arcades of knowing split from understanding and. the continuity we. temp. late. the sense of when i was young and when i will die as if the continuity of myself sustains a narrative

ageing in a line across time as if time were space to move across and as if i was something other than the continual death and rebirth of the always becoming i stamped I to constitute fabrications of mini-me a max cohesion. sold. my discontinuous I misunderstood by me as my continuity. I the intervention in a continuity of time as infinite simultaneity or the cosmic moss of geese or shrubs or maritime pine the above-surface green a shine of whirligig beetle carrying a handgun below the duckweed nudging always some bbq of unquiet multitude, those membranous confusions on the grill and through. and here we are with timelines, placing ourselves into a career of living. clocking on and off. signing on and off. but it continues. even when the world is burning with more fiercely imminent finality than our current crisis

there will be mutable makings and unmakings that will not concern us. maybe. and maybe when. and maybe when your device broadcasts the position of your device as the location of your being, sitting down to an over-documented pizza at an over-priced restaurant, underprepared for those cold homely spores becoming the outline of your passage through time, so much so that, on dying, the fixity of advertised memories betray any breath or essence with 'that moment when' you disconnected and joined the anonymous storage without depth of our species as it disappears into its own surveillance. smart. rubbles us and all that is gone. archives not of what was but of what it was we were taught to want. archives that archive themselves with the insistence on what can be caught. behavioural data as prediction. you identify with economic imperatives. the measurement of. net. the presentation of. work.

length and distance as the qualification of movement. listen to the numbers as they listen to who. codes choose war before conversation as you choose from the already chosen how best to reaffirm your absent choice. can any of this be left behind if what inhabited its purpose and perpetuated its use was first vacated by the terms of that use. you were left behind from being left behind. malignant frisbee and the cyst of. it gets mixed up. accelerating posed versions of a future past until nobody is present. this a past that never was. they combed us. it was us. we agreed with it. greedy for neighbourly contagion. became our own erasure until we had no memory of what was lost. we were but only in their memory. we couldn't tell ourselves apart from them and that was what we had. programmed. at the start. we didn't know how much we knew. although there were old phrases, always are, that said and say 'with one leg in the past and one in the future, you're pissing on the present' and yet, there is also the inability to conceive of a present without reference to a past through which, between memory and perception, action is realised for survival, and why would we strive to survive if not for the future. but some of us. some of us learnt to watch the movement.

learnt to stop searching for our own rubble. our rubble had been owned, but not by us and not as rubble. it was us. it was hard to tell. lifted from us without us but recorded from. seen. measured. enhanced. diminished. rubbles us and all that is gone. with water on my toes, cold. to be but washed up from. water now. as with is. the light. just now. you are a child. you see the sky playing in the water. i that am. it changes you. you see it change.

not as other but another

you. i am. it changes. skin feels how each hair lifts to meet the chill. how moving wills moving through. am. and you reach. changing. the sky. seeing am. from the ruins of searching for ruins freed. am now seeing. notice the way the water sounds when tilting the head, when the eyes close and open. moving out into it. how temperature. joy in the body's acceptance of cold. breathing that moves into. all rush of break spreads apart together in seen and unseen depth returning as turning the droplets up through air and down for rolling skin of height's blood quenching drawn of a moon as under a sun and above fires of earth that fall and rise carving volumes around endless bodying without body. tide happening to be. duration at once. noticing, beneath water as the light is changing. a stone.

Acknowledgements

I would like to thank the editors of *The Abandoned Playground, Shuddhashar* and *Volume,* for kindly including some of these poems in their magazines. I'd also like to thank my Dad, for a conversation in Edinburgh in which the detritus of not knowing began to fall more favourably. Sincere gratitude to the friendship and support of Daniel Bryden, John Challis, SJ Fowler, Wendy Heath, Kris Johnson, Julia Rose Lewis, Peter Manson, Jonnie McAloon, and Andrew Wells. Thanks to Emily, for new ways. Finally, I'd like to extend my deep thanks and admiration to the warmth and inspiration of Aaron Kent and for all the generous work of Broken Sleep Books.

lay out
your
unrest